Leading Through Living:

A Guide for Women Seeking Growth Through Leadership

Lynita Mitchell-Blackwell

ISBN: 978-0-9891457-2-5, 978-0-9891457-1-8

Dedicated to the Women in My Life

This book is dedicated to the women in my life who encouraged me to be the woman I am today: my mother Patience C. Mitchell; aunt Jessie C. Jenkins; mother-in-law Donna M. Blackwell; sister Patricia A. Mitchell; daughter, precious little princess Angelica; and my mentor Jewell Jackson McCabe.

Special Appreciation to the Men in My Life

My loving husband Brian K. Blackwell who never complained about interrupting his sleep with my 4:30am wake ups to write this book; father Bryon L. Mitchell who supported me through every endeavor and change it took to acquire the experience to write this book; proud father-in-law Dalden Blackwell who could not stop smiling when he heard the book was finished; and nephew Justin whose candid inquiry as to my book's completion status kept me going: "Are you finished yet?"

A world of thanks to my editor Kathryn V. Stanley for the fastest editing job in history.

Contents

Preface

We all have to go through something, but if your journey can be even a little easier learning from my adventures, then it makes my life experience that much better.

I have been mentally writing this book for at least six years. I started when I was president of a women's advocacy organization and noticed many of the women who gravitated toward leadership roles shied away from the consistent work and planning it takes to remain an effective leader. I was very fortunate to have a mentor who was honest and direct in her feedback with me. I realize now that her accessibility extended beyond that normally found in a mentor-mentee relationship. I largely credit her for many of the risks I have taken since serving in that post because she was so candid and gracious in sharing her life experiences. While I had all this wonderful information moving around inside me, I did not yet have the conceptual framework to succinctly package it or the practical experience to make it "mine".

Fast forward to present day. A law practice, family, and several leadership positions later, I found myself at a rare moment in life where everything was silent and I could hear myself think. I used that moment to ask myself, "So what now?" and really listen to the answer. The next day, I attended a vision board creation session and it all just came rushing out: NEXT! And within the "next" came the idea for this book. I came home from that session fired up and ready to go! I did not create an outline, plan each chapter, or consult with friends and colleagues about the content of the book. Rather, I sat down and wrote from my heart the things that I have learned through the years from working with great people just like you. I couched it as a leadership book for women because I am a woman. But truly this book has information that almost anyone may find valuable.

I have had, and continue to have, a wonderful life full of opportunities to work with different people on a myriad of projects — both paid and pro bono (or volunteer). It is these experiences that have shaped me into the person I am today, and I freely share these experiences with you. I worked very hard to ensure this book would not be too long so you enjoy it until the end. (I am guilty of starting self-help and guidance books, only to skim the last few sections.) I also focused on only sharing experiences that either I went through, personally witnessed, or were shared by reputable persons so that you are not bombarded with stories that may or may not have been entirely accurate.

I ask that you keep an open mind, use the information in this book to live a rich and rewarding life, and help others do the same. If something does not apply to you, that is okay – it may help someone else. If something really touches you – tell me about it. I would love to hear from you.

Let us begin!

The Great Choreographer

I recently attended an Alvin Ailey dance company performance that literally took my breath away. The dancers were incredibly gifted, their bodies literally floating through the air with a grace and rhythm that I can only dream of having in another life – if I am so lucky. I thoroughly enjoyed the performance for a number of reasons, but the one that stands out most in my mind was the way the dancers all worked together.

In any activity that involves more than one person, there will be a point where the nuances of our individuality come into play. Such is only natural and expected because we are individually working to do one thing. For instance, the Alvin Ailey artists were all completing the same dance move, but it performed slightly differently from one person to the next. Although barely perceptible, the slight variation made the performance unique and ensured that it would have a different feel each time the piece was performed. The choreographer knew this, and it was a major consideration in how she chose to cast the dancers. I witnessed true artistry.

Every group project should be like a well choreographed dance. As a leader, you are the choreographer; it is your job to determine where each person fits into the project based on their abilities (or how they move). Determining roles can be a challenge because some people are harder to read than others, but think of it as a joy to have the opportunity to work with people with various gifts to create something masterful and unique. Each person on your team is trusting that you have her best interests in mind, and will trust you to place her in the role that will not only showcase her talents, but also help prepare her for the next great opportunity in her career.

As in anything, you must be prepared for the initial rough start. When you begin working with a new team, even if you have worked together before, you must be prepared for the ramp up time that will initially affect negatively your productivity. Start up time should always be at the forefront of your mind as you set benchmark and completion goals. Be optimistic, but realistic. How? By trusting that you have the foresight and the experience necessary to select the right people (if that is within your control) or to get them in a place where they will be the right people (through coaching, training, and additional assistance if necessary) to get the project done right, on time, and in a way that makes everyone shine.

I know these seem like lofty goals, and they are. Goals should be realistic, yet stretch your current capacity (skills, knowledge, and resources) to force you to change and grow. If your goals, dreams, and ambitions do not challenge you, then they are not lofty enough. The same is true for your group. If the task is not big enough to push all of you to be better, then it is not big enough.

I know you must be thinking to yourself, "I'm not trying to stress myself out! Some goals have to be managed so that I have easy 'wins' that encourage me to push on." Yes, that is true, but managed goals lead to anticipated success, and anticipated success is not what will differentiate you from others who do what you do, and therefore will not get you where you want to be. Those who truly excel and shine work to accomplish not only what is expected (because you must at least do that so you may continue in your role), but the outstanding achiever also does the unexpected – the "shock and awe" factor. It can be as small as sending Thanksgiving holiday cards as everyone else sends cards a month later, or it can be as big as inviting the national founder of your organization to make the appeal for your individual chapter's giving goals to the local community.

Whatever you do, do it with all the style and pizzazz of a Broadway performance. That way, long after you are gone, the crowd will still be talking about it.

Shared Experience

A few years ago, I was invited to membership in a women's organization by a fellow law colleague. The organization's mission on paper was advocacy, but in reality was social. The conflict between the actual and apparent missions led to conflict in the membership. After about a year, I was elected president and decided to set the organization on to the path of advocacy. I reached out to the national founder who enthusiastically shared information and resources to make that happen. I used her materials as a guide to create a framework for our local community and the issues we faced, and then reviewed the experience and skills of my members to determine where they should serve and how they would personally benefit from serving in the selected role.

Once each person was appointed or elected, we got to work. It

8

was grueling in the beginning. Some people were very resistant to the change in our structure – they had only joined to have parties and attend VIP events, not work on social issues such as financial literacy. Others were afraid – this was all new and they had never served on any committee and here I was asking them to lead one. But we pushed through, and at the end of the first year, we had more than quadrupled our membership. At the end of the second year we had the third largest chapter in the national organization, and the incoming national president used our chapter as a model of advocacy for other chapters to follow.

None of this would have been possible without vision and trust. We shared a vision that we could do something great if we worked together. The membership trusted that I had each person's best interests at heart when I asked them to serve in various roles. And I trusted in myself and my abilities to do something that I had never done before and to lead others to do the same.

All these moving parts of the machine sometimes had me ready to pull my hair out and truly strengthened my prayer life. But it was an experience that has aided me in every role in which that I have served since, and I would not trade it for the world.□

Embrace All That Comes Your Way

"Absorb yourself in love, grace and gratitude each and every moment!" – Deidre N. Williams, Founder & CEO, The Protocol Academy

Our whole lives we are taught to avoid pain. As toddlers, we are taught not to touch the hot stove. As small children, we are taught to avoid bullies. As teens, we are taught to select classes in which we will excel and therefore boost our grade point averages. We take these lessons into adulthood which results in our taking risk-averse action that impact our ability to do truly marvelous, impactful things.

"Life is for the living," my mother always says. But how can you live if you do not fully embrace every experience – good or bad – that comes your way? If you are always looking for the easy way to do things, always avoiding conflict, or always tip-toeing around tough decisions, you will never grow. And if you do not grow, you will eventually become stagnant and your leadership abilities become dated, limited, and soon obsolete.

As our bodies grow, our muscles stretch over our bones due to the constant friction and tension this natural process requires. The same is true about your character growth and development. You must embrace the tension that naturally follows from new experiences, working with new people, and trying new things. We typically shy away from things with which we have limited or no experience, or where there is the faintest possibility of embarrassment or defeat. But these experiences are actually the most valuable because the lessons learned from them are long-lasting. The human mind remembers incredibly good things and extremely bad things, but we sort of filter out the things in the middle. Because we are human, we typically avoid any possibility of hurt and pain by removing ourselves from situations that we think may cause it or by building a wall around ourselves. Being impervious to pain is a limiting action. For pain and discomfort prompt us to move and to do something we would never have dreamed of doing.

Shared Experience

I recently spoke with a friend who shared the story of the founding of her company. She had a very good job with a stable firm in a professional office making good money. Then the economy tanked and she was unexpectedly laid off after eight years. She was a good saver, so the first year of unemployment was not so uncomfortable. But once the savings were gone, things became very tough. My friend started looking within herself for the things that she liked to do, and started a personal assistant company helping others with the things they like doing least. She began with one client - a member of her church - and a favor from a kind copy store employee who gave her business cards and brochures. Then she attended free conferences and talked about her business, promoting her usefulness and necessity for her services. One client became three, became ten, became a full time job that paid her bills and fulfilled her desire to be her own boss. None of this would have happened had it not been for the pain of losing her job and burning through her savings. You must understand – my friend is a very proud person, and she would have died before asking someone to give her anything. But she asked that copy store employee for the business cards on credit because she did not have the money to pay for them. And she leveraged her church member's referral to gain other clients through self promotion – something that she had previously disdained – because it was necessary to pay her bills.

It is hard to see the good as we go through challenging times such as the situation described above; but we must learn to analyze the thoughts and emotions that we experience through them, and use our challenges to put energy into positive, focused thinking and directed action. It is only then that we can come up with the solution to our problem and move past it.☐

Delay Is Not Denial

"No does not always mean no. Sometimes it simply means 'not yet'." --*Kimberly Esmond Adams, Superior Court Judge, Fulton County, Georgia*

It is amazing how comfortable we get in our routines and patterns, even when we are uncomfortable with the result of those actions. For example, when I think of the times I was hungry during a diet and reached for a fruit tart instead of a food that I suspected was good for me, I was simply operating in my zone of comfort. I knew that tart would not do anything for my weight loss goals and ate it anyway, increasing the amount of cardio I would need to do just to stay at par.

We do the same things in life, taking familiar action on items instead of a different action to get different results. Have you ever received a request and felt compelled to respond because you felt it was the "right thing to do," but not necessarily the right thing for you? I will challenge you to the following: the next time that happens, delay your response. You are not saying "no" and you are not ignoring the request, you are simply saying "not yet" or "I'm not prepared to respond right now." That is perfectly acceptable, particularly if your response would be a promise that you know you are not in a position to keep. Credibility is a huge part of strong leadership, and keeping your word proves credibility. It is better to hold off on a response and be able to commit to what you have promised than to promise something in the heat of the moment, but then disappoint.

Shared Experience

I recently had an exchange with a girlfriend where I asked her help in scheduling a meeting in a city where she lived that I would visit in two months. She said that she would be happy to offer her work space, but they were having a conference that day. When I asked if changing the meeting to another date would mean the space would be available, she did not respond. I did not take her lack of response as being unprofessional or unreliable. Rather, I believe she needed to do a bit of investigation and deliberate on the request.

You see, sometimes it is easy to respond to certain things because we know the barriers that exist – in this instance, there was already a function taking place, so that option was not available – it was entirely out of her hands. However, when I countered with another date that required a bit of research: Is something going on that is not on the calendar? Would it be alright to invite this (my) organization into the building? What are the parameters for such a meeting since it is technically not affiliated with the organization? Is there a charge for such a request?

Now, I will say a response at some point will be necessary – but sometimes the response is none at all. If time constraints require a quick response, then a lapse of the deadline answers that question. It would be nice to respond to a person in such a situation as quickly as possible, but not if it would put you in a compromising situation. You know the old saying, "A lack of planning on your part does not constitute an emergency on mine." If you can help the person, then do it. It will make you feel good. But if your involvement will require a huge sacrifice that leaves you feeling frustrated and unappreciated, then decline to get sucked in.

If you really want to continue to grow as a leader, you must be prepared to respond to people in a way that makes you feel empowered, not taken advantage of or your kindness abused. Sometimes such a response requires you to say "no", "not yet", or nothing at all – right now. You are not a bad person because you need to delay, you are a person who knows her commitments and strives to do her best with the 24 hours she was given in her day. And, you do not owe anyone an apology for that.

No Pain, No Gain

"In order to get something, you've got to give something." — Betty Wright, "No Pain, No Gain"

We naturally avoid uncomfortable situations and conversations because we generally like peace. We allow some things to slide, such as sly comments, and we allow other things to sit undone by those who should be doing them like un-made beds. Depending on the situation, these things taken individually are small and we deem them as not worth the time or effort to raise a fuss. However, taken over time and compounded with other frustrations, these same individually insignificant instances can become mountains of unresolved conflict.

Most people are familiar with the term "conflict management." It refers to several methods of resolving discord in groups that include avoidance, yielding, competing, cooperating, and conciliation. Before any of these methods may be utilized, one must face the problem to resolve it. This is where many leaders fail.

Discord is a natural state of affairs. Whenever there are two or more gathered, there will be competing thoughts and opinions. Some people just choose not to offer a difference of opinion, but it does not mean that they do not have one. Remember, most people simply want to get along, but that is not what promotes or sustains growth and success. As a leader, you must cultivate an environment where diverse thoughts are encouraged and welcomed so that "group think", meaning everyone in the group thinks alike or no one or only a few people think for themselves, does not set in. Group think leads to lack of competitiveness and eventually irrelevance.

A thriving environment in which diversity of thought and action is accepted is one based on mutual respect. You must set the tone for such acceptance by encouraging your team and colleagues to voice their thoughts with spirit but not obnoxiousness; challenging information in a manner that is cordial and based on fact not emotion; allowing people to "get it all off their chests" so that all the passion has been expended; and finally, decisively ruling on an issue in a manner that conveys you have taken all that was shared into account and explaining why you are taking the chosen position.

The explanation for your actions is key for both you and for your team. You need to believe what you are doing with all your being to give your best effort, even when you get tired and/or are no longer so passionate about the end goal or both. You also need a road map showing from idea, discussion to decision, so that if conditions upon which you based your decision change, you can quickly change direction without going through the entire pow-wow session again.

The explanation is important to those who follow you so that they know you heard what they said, took it into consideration, and respect them enough to articulately and intelligently convey their thoughts back to them. Many times, people do not expect you to do everything they suggest, but knowing that you thought enough to listen and consider their thoughts is more than they could have asked.

Shared Experience

I have a client who is also a very dear friend who showed me the value of all of the above. She started a behavioral health organization that she made profitable within 18 months through hard work and very hard knocks. Her first partner put her through hell and we spent many days talking through the frustration of that experience that eventually led to the partner's buyout.

A year later, my friend and client was ready to take on a new partner. I immediately balked for several reasons, but there were two prime ones. The first was that she had built the business to a $1M company within three years by herself and I believed she did not need the headache of another person disrupting her "groove." Second, the person she identified was qualified as far as skills and character, but did not bring any capital to the table. I believed the person she identified should have been promoted to vice-president and given stock options, but not full partnership. My client listened to my concerns, thought seriously about them, but ultimately decided to bring the person on as a partner.

When she told me her decision, she was kind, yet firm. She was moving and wanted to leave the business in capable hands that had a vested interest in not only managing but growing the business. The person she identified was trustworthy and loyal – not only was he an employee, but also a good friend. And this person had very strong analytical skills that had lead to excellent inspection and quality review scores. She thanked me for my advice, but asked me to move forward drafting the partnership agreement so that the capital the person was bringing to the table was his experience and network. Although I disagreed with my client, I appreciated that she explained her position, and did as she asked.

Of course, she was my client and I did what she asked because I was paid to do so. But I did so without grudge and did not feel that my time had been wasted in preparing my recommendation. And, because I did not feel disrespected, when an opportunity came to my attention to help my friend and client – that would not benefit me in any way – I was happy to pass it along.

Some of the best ideas come from brainstorming sessions where people with different life experiences come together for one purpose. Do not avoid working with people that see things differently or because there may be friction that results in that meeting. Take it all the way, push past the hard part. There is reward for those who stick it out, and this is no exception. If you think of the child-birthing experience, labor is one of the most excruciatingly painful experiences in life, but the joy that follows when the child arrives far surpasses the pain. No pain, no gain. □

Live for Today

"If we wait until we're ready, we'll be waiting for the rest of our lives." — Lemony Snicket

My mother always says, "life is for the living." It is imperative that we live the best life we can, every moment of every day because tomorrow may never come. I know that sounds a bit morbid, but it is actually quite liberating. Just think – if you did everything you wanted to do today without fear of what tomorrow's consequence would be, your every action and thought would resonate power and authority! You would not think small, limiting thoughts about how you're not ready for "that" now. You would not waste energy working on a project you know is a non-starter. You would not wait for the next best thing – you would get to work making it happen.

I recently had dinner with a dear friend who is self conscious about her size. I have known her since college, and both of our waist lines have expanded over the years. We were celebrating her birthday and we took a picture that she refuses to post or share – anywhere – because she "needs to lose weight." She is beautiful – both inside and out – no matter her size, and I told her so. But my words meant nothing because she was determined to wait until she was perfect (i.e., until she lost weight) to share the pictures from her special day.

As leaders, we are taught to do our best every time, work hard at everything we do, and to present our best face at all times. I believe in that mantra, but there is a part to that we need to discuss a bit: our best changes over time depending on our state of wellbeing. How we feel about life in general, and particular parts of life specifically, affect how we perform and our energy levels, appearance, and self-confidence. Our mental, physical, and emotional states change over time for various reasons such as environment, relationship status, parenting status, changes in job or locale, friendship renewal and/or loss, loss of a loved one, schedule conflicts, and on and on and on. We deal with these things differently as time goes on – how we deal with a difficult manager in our 20's is different than how we deal with such a person in our 30's. Hopefully, we deal with things better as we get older, but age and experience do not necessarily transcend into positive actionable results. Rather, it is our ability to see ourselves as powerful and in control of our destiny at all times that gives us the strength and fortitude we need to navigate life's ups and downs.

Did you know that many women do not run for office because they are waiting for the "right time"? I participated in a political training for women a few years ago, and the facilitator told us that the difference between men and women as potential candidates was not education, talent, connections, or finances – it was perspective. She shared that a guy will wake up wearing a t-shirt and shorts with no job or prospects whatsoever and say to himself "I'm going to run for office!" and do it. A woman in a similar position would say to herself "After I get a job, save some money, get active in the community, get the children settled, and help my husband get situated, then I will run for office" and 20 years go by before she even considers taking action.

Both examples are extreme, but the point the facilitator was trying to make was that we cannot wait for everything to be perfect in life for us to decide to pursue our dreams and live the best life we can today. Every person gets the same 24 hours in a day and it is imperative that we use each moment wisely. Do not avoid speaking opportunities because you feel you are not a subject matter expert – focus your mind on learning what you need to know so you can bring the noise at that next seminar! Say "YES" the next time someone asks you to serve as lead on a project, even if you have not led a team before – everyone had a first day doing everything they do well now. No person came straight from the womb fully formed and ready to go. Pose for pictures, even if you are having a "bad hair day" – memorialize your accomplishments and travels for positive reflection later. Try new things now, today, this instant – you have nothing to lose because what you are trying you do not have anyway. You have everything to gain whether it is experience on how to do it better next time or gratefulness when it all turns out fine. Seize the day!

The Power in Mistakes

"No one should be ashamed to admit they are wrong, which is but saying, in other words, that they are wiser today than they were yesterday."—Alexander Pope

Each day we draw breath, we will make a mistake. The error may be something as small as not responding to a "thank you" or as grave as an action resulting in bodily injury. Life is filled with opportunities to do good work, but it is also ripe with temptation to take short cuts and be small minded. We have all at one time offended someone, done something that we knew was wrong, or failed to take action when it was clear that we were the only ones who had the power to ensure the right outcome. I would love to tell you that these instances will disappear over time, but that is just not true. But I can tell you that as you learn to take more time to respond to people, plan for events, and take notice of your surroundings, these instances will occur less frequently.

Your ability to own up to your mistakes, apologize as soon as possible once you have realized them, and learn from the experience is critical to your success – or failure – as a leader. People follow people they respect. A person who is confident in her abilities and her ability to take responsibility for all of her actions is someone for whom many people would march over a cliff. That kind of devotion is reserved for those who earn it. You earn it by learning from your errors and sharing that knowledge with others.

Shared Experience

I was an executive recruiter for about a year, and during that time I worked with a tax manager whose resume was solid on experience but short on stability. She had a great personality, and I agreed to work with her over the objections of my manager. I placed her at a Fortune 100 company within two weeks and was flying high. But then she started acting flaky about the salary – the same salary I had told her about before the interview, that the company told her about during the interview, and the same salary that was presented in her offer letter. Needless to say, she withdrew her acceptance of the job. The client thought I had not vetted the candidate, and declined to view any other candidates I referred for that position.

I was very upset by that experience and stewed for days. In reflecting on the entire situation, I decided that I needed to do three things: apologize to my manager for not respecting his concerns about the candidate's background; apologize to the client for wasting a month of their time; and share my experience with my co-workers so they would not repeat my mistake.

I apologized to my client and they agreed to allow me to refer candidates for other positions within the company. I apologized to my manager, and he suggested that I make it up to him by leading a training for new recruiters. I decided to use the training to accomplish my third goal which was to share my experience with that candidate.

I showed them that candidate's resume, pointing out the strengths that included her experience and specialized knowledge in very technical tax areas. I also showed them the challenges of the resume that included poor job stability and excessive contracting with companies that had full time positions available in the areas she had worked. I also shared how I made the decision to work with the candidate, the most compelling being that she was getting older and wanted a stable position with benefits. I went on to tell them what I would have done differently to not only better vet the candidate, but also to properly manage severed communication with client.

After the training, the new hires sought me out for advice and guidance when confronted with challenges, both small and large. It made me feel good that they valued my opinion, and respected my counsel. But most importantly, I learned the value of sharing both good and bad experiences.

Just Try

"Be willing to be wrong, and know that — whatever the consequences — you'll survive." –Iyanla Vanzant

Sometimes we hesitate to try something new because we fear failing. Do not let your fears paralyze you and keep you from reaching up and out for your dreams. You must try new things to gain the varied experience and wisdom you will need to move to the next great thing in your life. This is true in your personal and professional relationships.

You are a strong, resourceful, smart, beautiful woman and I believe you have the fortitude to deal with whatever comes your way. And trust and believe that as you become more successful, more challenges will come your way. I believe the world is perfectly balanced between good and bad. Life is like that — have you noticed that when one area of your life takes off another falls apart? We strive for perfection in all aspects of our lives, and we should continue to do so because the effort is what makes us strong and brings value to our experiences. However, we should always remember that perfect balance will never be achieved. Why? Because no one and no-thing is perfect. There is nearly perfect, almost perfect, but never absolutely perfect.

One thing I do everyday no matter how I feel or what is going on is mentally replay the refrain from my favorite song "Get Up" by Mary Mary. It encourages me to get up, get moving, and put forth my best effort – just try! I instantly feel better and a surge of energy races through me. Momentum is important to your success, but so too is consistency, and it is imperative that you develop methods to keep you going so you may continue to put forth the necessary effort to achieve everything you put your mind to.

Another thing I do to keep me going is stay in constant communication with my girlfriends. I have two who I speak with almost every day. When I do not speak with them, the world just does not feel the same. We talk about everything, and it makes all the difference in the world that I have a sounding board and nurturing environment where I can share my hopes and my fears. These ladies know me inside and out, and we have an unspoken but clearly respected rule that we are honest with one another – no matter what.

Shared Experience

I received an email from a colleague soliciting candidates to run for president of a state professional organization that I had not been a member of for two years. The current president was moving and no one from the existing membership wanted to serve. I pondered the email for a couple of days, turning around in my mind the possibility of serving in such a high profile role. The timing was perfect: I had just rolled off two other boards, my daughter was in school, and my practice was doing fine. But I was afraid. I knew only a handful of the current membership, I had never served as president of a professional organization and certainly not one so large, and I was not sure I would do a good job.

Enter my girlfriends! They both encouraged me to run. One told me that I would be fine because she knew I would enjoy the challenge of learning a new way of leading. The other told me I was doing more than anyone else was willing to do, and the support would come from the membership just to ensure the responsibility stayed with me and did not pass to one of them. So I renewed my dues, ran, and won. I got to work immediately mapping out ways to recruit new members and reclaim old ones, identifying opportunities to work with other professional organizations, and setting the meeting schedule so we would have time to network and share resources. And you know both of my girlfriends were right! The enthusiasm I showed in getting to work and personally reaching out to every member of the association was contagious, and we were up and thriving in a couple of months.

I learned one of the most valuable lessons imaginable that day: you do not have to know everything to inspire people; they will be willing to help you once they see you out there working.

Making the "Right" Decision

"I would rather be strongly wrong than weakly right." —Tallulah Bankhead

Being an effective leader requires decisive action. Sometimes we are required to make decisions quickly, and other times we have the luxury of thoughtful deliberation. In either case, we are expected to make a choice and stick to it. This type of thinking is very "black or white," and nothing is ever that "cut and dried" as my mother would say. To be a leader people love to follow, you must learn to be flexible. Not a person who straddles the fence, but one who will make a better decision when presented with better information.

Why is this important? First, no one person is perfect, and to believe that you will always make the best decision the first time is incredibly naïve. Do you remember your first day of work? Did you know enough to set the world on fire on day one? Of course not! Although you are far removed from that first day perhaps having received awards and recognition, and made contributions to your organization, the same principle still applies: As you learn and grow, so too will your perspective and experiences that influence your decision making process and color your ultimate outcome.

Second, while your core values do not change over time, your opinions certainly do. Opinions about people and their motives, our community and its needs, and our desire for and methods to achieve fulfillment change with time. Therefore, our decision making process changes as well. Don't believe me? When you go out to eat, do you quickly review what you had earlier that day to determine what you will eat right now? I bet you did not do that when you were 10 – you simply ordered what you wanted (French fries and hamburgers!). Now, you would probably order a salad and baked chicken. As an adult, you make better food choices than when you were a child because your taste buds have developed and you have experienced different types of cuisine. Similarly, as an ever progressing leader, your mind is exposed to and dissects new thoughts, trainings, books, and ways of doing things and filters those new ideas directly into your decision making process ultimately impacting your conclusions.

Third, being an effective leader with staying power requires you to work with different people differently, and to do so graciously. To accomplish this, you must be willing to hear other people's perspectives on what is to be done, and to take their thoughts and feelings into consideration before you act. Now let us be clear: this does not mean you must cow-tow to every person in the room, practice quid pro quo with other persons in leadership, or bend to the will of any one person just to keep the peace. Rather, it means that you must listen – truly hear what others are saying – and respect the opinions of others, acknowledge their expression, and make the decision that you can zealously defend when called on the carpet. Notice that I did not say "live with," I said "zealously" defend – vigorously, passionately, and intelligently stand by your decision. This is necessary because at the end of the day, it is you who will have to answer for the consequences of the decision – good or bad. Just as in anything else, since you are the head, all eyes are on you – in good times and bad.

So instead of focusing on making the "right" decision, try instead to make the best decision. That way, you can state your position with conviction, yet have room to pivot later if or when better information becomes available.

You Don't Have to Know Everything

"When you know better you do better." – Maya Angelou

There is great courage in deferring to someone else's expertise and wisdom when you are the one ultimately responsible. Great leaders do it every day, such as our president who relies on his advisors and Cabinet members. Because we are perfectionists, and we think about all the things that can go wrong if the decision is the "wrong" one, we resist asking for help or accepting it even when we know the person offering is doing so with pure motives with the ability and skill to guide us well. Here is a way to alleviate your angst in accepting help: compromise - with yourself.

In exchange for you asking and accepting a consultation on this matter, you promise to learn all you can during the process to be well-versed on the points you believe you are weakest on. This way, you do not feel that things are going over your head, and if pressed on a particular topic, you will feel comfortable responding. In the meantime, learn to become comfortable giving the wheel to someone better equipped to "drive the bus" as you are traveling down the road. Once you reach the outskirts of the destination city, you can re-take the wheel and lead the group the rest of the way. And remember, give an appropriate nod of appreciation to the person who helped get you to your destination.

Shared Experience

I served as chairperson of a non-profit board. During a meeting as we were going through the agenda, one of the board members corrected me on a motion citing parliamentary procedure. I had never heard the motion stated the way she said it, but was not a Robert's Rules expert and did not have my manual with me, so I deferred to her on the matter. I must admit that when we used the motion, it cut down on time and we were out of the meeting pretty quickly. I thanked my colleague after the meeting and promised myself to learn more about parliamentary procedure.

When I got home, I reviewed my rule book and saw the motion

to which she referred and learned to use it. Although my colleague actually instructed me to use the motion incorrectly, I was glad the issue came up because it forced me to bone up on my parliamentary procedures and to carry Robert's Rules from that point forward.

Before we began our next meeting, I laughingly told the board that I had a copy of Robert's Rules and was ready this week, and thanked my colleague on the use of that motion. I also explained how the motion was to be used, and when it was appropriate to use it. I did not blast her in front of everyone about her incorrect instruction because the point was not to embarrass anyone, it was to ensure that everyone had the knowledge I had. It went over fine; two members laughed and said that the experience made them start carrying their Rules books, too.

We Have Not Because We Ask Not

"Pride cometh before destruction." —Proverbs 16:18

Most people strive to do things well most of the time. As an ambitious person, you probably strive to do things perfectly all the time. Not only is perfection impossible, it also limits to your development into the best leader you can be.

Every group has a leader, whether that person is explicitly or implicitly selected. But the key word here is "group" – it takes more than one person to bring about the best outcome in any situation. Yes, there is always the most valuable player or MVP, but that person's value is determined by her performance when compared to others. It is the MVP's privilege to work within the group that allowed her to shine. Without the group, the MVP would never have developed the skills necessary to perform with such distinction.

Did you ever wonder how a person transitioned from average to excellent? It takes courage to overcome challenges and adversity, determination not to sink into despair, and faith that things will get better. It also takes asking others to help when things become too much to bear.

Take a moment to reflect on your challenges and struggles. When you were down, did you just sit there and wait for the situation to pass or did you do something? I bet you did something, starting with talking about it with someone you trusted. Once you talked your situation through, you were able to see things a bit differently, even seeing things that had previously been obscured by your closeness to the situation. And your confidant probably offered you some advice or assistance to aid you in your time of need. But you would not have been able to obtain this help if you had not shared your story.

Because we do so many things exceedingly well, successful women view the need to share and ask for help as a form of weakness. It is not; it is a sign of great strength and strong character to own your vulnerability. No person was born to live alone in this life. It takes two parents to create a child, a mother and baby to achieve birth, one must be taught to care for one's self, and so on.

Just because we become adults and physically independent does not make us emotionally or mentally separate from the rest of the world. As we get older, we should want to connect more with others so we may continue to learn from them and grow with them. It is only through this shared sense of being that we realize our ultimate purpose and potential.

Pride is a great thing when taken in stride. It compels us to demand to be treated with respect and dignity, present ourselves neatly and professionally, produce exceptional work, and work to be the best we can be. But we must be careful not to allow our pride to cut us off from the world, making it seem impossible to ask for help. Our friends and colleagues are more than happy to assist us, and we must allow them to do so. It robs them of the opportunity to show us how much they care about us and to learn different skills in assisting us.

Sometimes, they may become annoyed at the lack of timeliness or specificity of our request for help; that is just fine, let them fuss and watch how they come to our aid anyway. What is a little nagging between friends?

Shared Experience

In writing this book, I experienced a joy and pride that made me smile each time I thought about the next chapter and the people who would read and enjoy it. When I finished my last sentence, I thought I was ready to go to straight to publication. I shared my joy with a girlfriend who listened patiently, and when I was finished, she gently but firmly told me that I had several steps to go before I was ready to unleash my work onto the world, most notably hiring an editor.

I was a little stunned. I am an attorney, have written various blog posts and articles, and really thought I did not need an editor. My friend explained to me that an editor is so much more than a proofreader – that person ensures the flow and evenness of one's work. I stewed a bit, but decided to accept her counsel in this because she has worked with other writers and this was my first time. I reached out to a former church member who I knew had prior editing experience and I am so glad I did! The information she shared was incredible and the value added noticeable.

Had I not been willing to put my pride to the side and allow a professional to help me, this book may not have come together as quickly or fluidly as it has. Thank goodness for candid friends.□

The Gilded Tongue

"Folks, there are three phrases that will get you farther in life than anything else you will ever learn: please, thank you, and excuse me." -the late Dr. Colin O. Benjamin, Tenured Professor of Engineering Management, Florida A&M University School of Business & Industry

The best advice I ever received has been related to civility and courtesy. The further along I get in my career – in my life in general – I appreciate even more the importance of treating people well. Peggy Parks, founder of The Parks Image Group and self-proclaimed Ambassador of Corporate Civility, has a weekly e-blast that touts the incredible impact that civility – or the lack thereof – can have on performance.

We are all smart, driven, connected and successful women. While these characteristics are important to our success, none of these are the determining factor in our ability to win people over. When you meet a person, they do not always know how important or smart you are, but they will immediately know how you treated them and whether they want to engage with you beyond what is absolutely necessary.

It is imperative to treat each person you meet with respect, and give them a chance to make a good impression. Shake a hand when it is offered, even if you are a germa-phobe – just carry antibacterial lotion. Smile and make eye contact with people when you speak with them. Say "excuse me" when you accidentally cut someone off mid-sentence. Offer to hold the door for the person behind you – that may be the very person you are about to meet. These suggestions may seem simplistic, but put yourself in the position of the person on the receiving end: How would you feel if you extended your hand to someone and they left you "hanging"? How would you feel if you were talking and the person to whom you are trying to convey your point was looking everywhere but at you? How would you feel if someone let the door slam in your face? Now imagine that same person has now come to ask for something. Would you be inclined to answer them favorably? Probably not.

Many of our decisions are made based on how we feel. Our performance in any given situation is impacted by our emotions. If bestowing a bit of kindness on to someone else would help that person feel good about you, and therefore view you more favorably, wouldn't you want that? Of course you would! And remember this – all things held equal, if a decision is to be made regarding a hire, purchase, or selection, people go with the person they like. (And sometimes they go with the person they like even when things are far from equal.)

Timely communication and response is also important in conveying to people how much we appreciate their time and effort. When someone calls you, listen to the voicemail before calling back. It could require a quick response that you can send back via voicemail, or a more detailed response you would prefer to send in writing via email. Either way, do your best to return the call by the end of the day. When someone emails you, thoroughly read it before you reply, and re-read it to ensure your reply has addressed the issue. This often avoids email chains with three or more responses that could have been addressed in one.

Shared Experience

I recently sent a request to a fellow attorney to speak at an event. I asked for a response within a week, but did not hear anything. I followed up with two other requests, again no response. Two weeks later, I received an email from her apologizing profusely for her delayed response and explaining that she had been out with the flu. Of course, I understood the delay in my colleague's response, and was relieved to know she was alright. Although that speaking opportunity had been filled, I promised her I would keep her in mind for future events. I was happy to do this because I knew that her lack of response was out of character based on her reputation as a courteous and respectful person.

Phone, Email & Text Communication

I would also encourage you to greet people in a friendly manner when you call or email. Our time is valuable and we like to handle issues as quickly and efficiently as possible, but we can do so in a courteous manner. Taking two or three seconds to begin a conversation with "Hello" or "How are you today?" will not kill you, but it will set a positive tone to the conversation that may have been lost if you had launched directly into it with "Did you make the deadline?"

One last thought on communication. Texting is great when we need a short, quick response to simple questions. But I would encourage you not to use this medium to discuss matters of import or those that require confidentiality or discretion. Many of us use short hand when texting, but it is not appropriate – or polite – to do so when we are trying to convey complex thoughts, ideas, or emotions. No matter how technologically advanced we become, some things should still be said in person – or not at all.

Appreciation

Always show your team members your appreciation. Do not undervalue the power of "please" and "thank you." When leading a project, initiative, group, or organization, people do what we task them with because that is what they are supposed to do. And when someone is supposed to do something, they typically only do the absolute bare minimum to get by. Try asking your team to do what you have placed on the to-do list: "Maggie, please do X by Y date." And thank the person upon completion with sincere praise: "Maggie, this is really good, thank you."

Notice I said "sincere praise". No one appreciates being made to feel that your praise is disingenuous. This undermines your credibility and influence, making it harder for you to get things accomplished. Remember, accomplishments are what drive your success.

Delivering Bad News

As a leader, you will find yourself delivering bad news – there is no avoiding it. No matter to whom I am sharing the unpleasant news, I always keep in mind that there is a human being with thoughts and feelings taking in what I am saying, and that I need to keep in mind that they are going to react to not only what I am saying, but how I am saying it.

One of the ways that I try to minimize the negative impact of bad news is to say it how I would want it said to me. Depending on the situation, I may ease into it (particularly if it is a friend); or I may say it directly and pause for response (in a business setting). I try to gauge the person's mood, as best I can, to determine the best way to say what needs to be said. I would encourage you to be respectful of the person by

- Saying what needs to be said honestly and forthrightly,
- Not abandoning the effort, leaving them wondering what is coming,
- Not saying it in a way that implies they were less than intelligent for not seeing it coming, and
- Not sending someone else to deliver the news.

One thing about wearing the "big girl skirt" is that you take the good and the bad together. Because you are out front, you get all the praise, accolades, and awards for the work you – and your team – accomplish together. So it follows that you must also take the criticism and impossible tasks that go with it.

Step Away... Move On

"Be right, be strong, be brief, be gone!" -the late Rev. Dr. G. L. Champion, Sr., former Director of Church Growth & Evangelism, AME Church and builder of multi-million dollar St Mark AMEC Orlando, a faith-based community center

As a successful woman who works hard to build great things, you are territorial and possessive about those things in which you have you invested so much. The investment is not just monetary – it is your time away from your business, time away from your family, leisure time forsaken in the name of perfection and the ultimate coup – praise and adoration. But these times do and must come to an end. And when they do, you must move on quickly, graciously, and completely. If you do not, you will become that person you so dislike – meddlesome, troublesome, critical, and negative. And you may not get a second chance to unring that bell – your credibility will be damaged, and your feelings irreparable hurt.

Consider this scenario: You've decided to take my challenge and assume leadership of an unknown organization that happens to be struggling. You spend a week reviewing past programs, talking with former members about what went right (and oh, so wrong) with the organization, creating new and exciting projects to re-engage the community and generate passion within your remaining members' hearts, and putting your own finances on the line to make all of this happen.

Fast forward nine months (yes, the time it takes to have a baby is about the time it will take to truly turn an organization around). The fledgling organization is now a thriving enterprise, full of enthusiastic and happy people, ready to work at a moment's notice. People are coming to you with ideas, and they cannot wait to receive the green light to go forth and prosper. So you unleash them, and the team thrives. They are making new contacts, identifying new opportunities for growth and partnership, talking about the organization in the community in a way that has others calling you with an almost envy in their voices as they congratulate you on a seemingly impossible job well done.

You are feeling good now! The harvest is bountiful, and you are reaping it. But just as each season has its start and end date, so too do you and your leadership. After a few short years, you start to feel a little burned out, people are not responding to you as quickly as they used to, or as enthusiastically as you thought they should. The same things that used to excite them – rewards, awards, recognition, new assignments – just do not work. You are a smart woman, so you know the warning signs: it is time to move on.

But you are scared. You spent so much time and effort building this initiative into what it is. No one else knows the ins and outs as well as you do. Plus, you believe if you are not involved, things will not get done as well as they could, so the organization will suffer. You do not want to leave before X thing is completed. And besides, what if the next person only wants the position for glory, not for service?

Guess what? All of this may be true, but I promise you, if you were to drop dead tomorrow, these same people you feel cannot live without you will mourn you... and move on! Did you get that? They will miss you, remember you fondly, but trust me, the show will go on. So instead of staying in a position past your expiration date, as my grandfather use to say, "Leave while the crowd is still cheering".

How do you do this? First, you should have identified at least two people who have the desire, ability, and intellect to lead in a positive manner a year before you began thinking of leaving. Remember, the grooming process does not start when you decide you are tired, rather, it begins when you get things under control.

Second, you must give the identified persons more responsibility and visibility to determine their fitness for the job. Some people do well when directed and led by others, but when given the freedom and responsibility to guide a group do not perform well at all. They may be intemperate, self-involved, or lack vision. Keep searching for your diamonds; they are out there.

Now that your protégés are out front, you must start to refocus your attention on "what's next?" for you. Are you going to

- Take some time off to reestablish relationships that probably languished while you were flying high?
- Work on new streams of income and ideas to improve your profitability?
- Explore new trainings and educational opportunities to

expand your knowledge base?
- Engage on a low level in some other project or organization, so you stay connected to others in your industry?

I hope the answer is "yes" to all of the above. Why? Because you need to decompress and de-stress. Working on any initiative requires energy and commitment, and you give more than most. You must take time after these incredible outputs of energy to recharge your batteries. If you do not give yourself time to heal, each subsequent commitment will get less effort than the last, until your best looks like half of how it used to look not too long ago.

Now that you have identified the next person, groomed her to take over, made your plan for "NEXT," it is time to exit stage left. How do you do that gracefully? Easy: just go. The organization – its people, leadership, or you – have selected or elected a successor. Your stepping away is simply a formality. Attend the farewell gala, attend the inauguration, and then attend to yourself:
- Refer all calls, text messages, emails, and snail mail to your successor.
- Ignore negative talk and complaints about your successor.
- Take compliments to your time in leadership in stride, but do not dwell on those times – focus on the future and talk about what you are doing now.
- Spend time with acquaintances not so involved in your old endeavor.
- Have fun – work on knocking off a couple of your bucket list items.

It will not be easy to watch the project you nurtured be tended to by someone else. You will always feel that there was something else you could have done, something else you should have tried, someone else you should have engaged, and that you should have hung in there a little longer. Those feelings will pass. Know that what you did was important, valued, and made the world better.

You are better for this experience, and now it is time to move on.

Shared Experience

I co-founded a leadership training organization few years ago along with three dynamic women. We all agreed that when it was time to move on, we would do so, but we did it incrementally so that the organization would not be without institutional knowledge. I was the last person to roll off, and it was very difficult. For four years, that organization had been my baby and I did not want her to grow up. But she had grown up – four divisions, 300+ national and international participants, and four graduating classes. It was time to turn the reigns over to the next set of leaders.

At first it was hard. The new leadership changed the training schedule, moved the fundraiser up two months, and replaced long standing partnerships with others. Persons with knowledge of these changes came to me in a panic, begging me to do something. I was tempted, but restrained myself by remembering the courtesy and respect shown to me when I transitioned into leadership of another organization. I used that as a model for my behavior in this one.

I said nothing negative, directed all detractors back to my successor, and continued to pursue my NEXT pursuits that included learning to use a firearm, Salsa dancing, and serving on two new boards. Although I do not agree with everything that has been done, I am so glad that I did not interfere and gave my successor a chance to make the organization stronger by shaking things up a bit. ☐

Make Regret an Unwelcome Visitor in Your Life

"View your life with kindsight. Stop beating yourself up about things from your past. Instead of slapping your forehead and asking, "What was I thinking," breathe and ask yourself the kinder question, "What was I learning?" — Karen Salmansohn, The Bounce Back Book: How to Thrive in the Face of Adversity, Setbacks, and Losses

Mistakes are part of living. If you are breathing, you will commit some error that wrongs someone else and/or yourself. There is no shame in making a mistake; the trouble comes in not knowing how to you handle it.

Some mistakes are small, and can be overcome with a simple "I am sorry". Others require corrective action. Those errors are relatively easy to overcome when compared to the mistakes we all dread: those that cannot be rectified by word or deed, but must be forgiven, let go, and allowed to pass. Forgiveness is a hard thing – it requires strength, courage, and vulnerability. I know the latter seems to be out of place here – vulnerability is not usually coupled with courage. However, true forgiveness requires one to face the possibility of the same disappointment.

The first thing to do in a situation where you have wronged someone is to determine how you got here and how it may be avoided in the future – i.e., what did you learn? And how may that knowledge aid you to ensure that "this" does not happen this way again?

Second, forgive yourself. You are allowed to forgive yourself before anyone else can. I would push further and say that you must forgive yourself before someone else can because you are the one experiencing discomfort, embarrassment, and guilt that color your actions. You must release them so they do not forever shade the light you bring into the world.

Next, ask the wronged party for forgiveness – and that wronged party may be you. Admit what you did, ask to be forgiven, and allow the other person to speak. We get into trouble here because we want so badly to explain why we did what we did and rationalize our behavior. Whatever it was, it was wrong, and you need to allow the person receiving her apology to digest what you have to say. Now understand, sometimes the person will need time depending on how egregious your behavior. (If you wrongly identified someone in a line up and they served 20 years in prison for a crime they did not commit, do not be surprised if it takes 20 years – or never – for you to receive any feedback.) You must be prepared for this and know that your absolution has to come from you. This is why you must first forgive yourself.

Last, accept the wronged party's position on how things stand and give them the space they need to move on in their lives. Every person comes into our lives for a reason, and it is our job to determine what it is. Some people are here forever, some only for a defined period of time. If the person from whom you seek forgiveness decides that they no longer want to be part of your life, embrace the good memories that came from the relationship, and accept and respect that person's decision.

Acceptance and respect are hard, particularly if the rift is between two people who have a deep bond of affection (not necessarily romantic, but one built on a solid track record of performance, overcoming adversity and challenge, and success). But showing the person that you are willing to abide by her decision is sometimes the best way of communicating that you have learned from your error, that to the best of your ability it will not happen again, that you are open to reconnecting at a later time if the person so chooses.

Shared Experience

When I was in college, I sent a letter to a (former) good friend criticizing her for various things. At the time, I felt justified because she had said some hurtful things to me and I was retaliating. Once I mailed it, I wanted to kick myself for being so mean. When she received the letter, she called and expressed her shock and anger. Instead of apologizing for my boorish behavior, I doubled down and reiterated my position. It did not end well.

Fast forward a few years. I attended a workshop where the facilitator encouraged us to think about a person we had wronged and what we would do if we had the chance to fix it. He then encouraged us to write the person a letter and send it to her if possible. I did, and when my former friend received, it she called me and we talked a long time. I apologized, but did not try to explain my behavior – the point was to let her know that what I had said was out of line and that I wished to make amends. She was very gracious and accepted my apology. We will probably never be as close as we were in college, but the fact that we are on good terms now is sufficient.

Plan, Save, Give...Live!

"Happiness is not something you postpone for the future; it is something you design into the present." — Myesha Waring Good, President, Democratic Women's Council of Douglas County, modifying original quote of Jim Rhon

As a person empowered to lead others, you have (or will) establish a brand of excellence and exceptionalism that translates as your unique signature. You put everything you have into your current project, bordering on tunnel vision. As conscientious people, we tell ourselves that everything must be perfect, therefore we work ourselves "to the bone" to ensure that perfection. But I would like to share something with you that came to me recently: you are not expected to give 100% to anything and you should not give everything to anyone. I know that sounds counterintuitive, but stay with me for a moment.

For those of you familiar with tithing and saving in the biblical context, one is expected to give 10%, save 10% and live on the rest – which is 80%. Using this as a model for leaders (and I believe it is safe to do so – some of the most revered leaders in history are those in the Bible who lived by these principles), that means you would:

- Give 10% of your time, talent and resources for faith building purposes.
- Save 10% of your time, talent and resources as reserve.
- Live in the now – truly the present - with the remaining 80%.

This is a real challenge in light of our busy lives. There are "only" 24 hours in a day to accomplish everything we place on our "to do" lists. But let me show you how you can be even more effective and productive using the 10-10-80 rule:

Give 10%. Give 10% of your efforts on a pro bono basis (or free) to causes and organizations that you care about. Many people give to their faith-based organization, be it their churches, synagogues, mosques, or other organized affiliation. Others give to community or donor driven organizations, such as the Red Cross, the American Cancer Society, or Girl Scouts. Find your passion and give with gusto!

Financial gifts are always needed and appreciated by these organizations. If you are in a position to donate monetarily, please do. I personally tithe and could go on for quite some time regarding the benefits of it. But community and civic organizations also need well trained volunteers who are willing to serve (not just be seen). This is the main reason it is important to volunteer with organizations whose mission and vision you agree with, and where you may be useful. If you do not believe – or have faith - that you are putting into the organization, you will fade away into the background and leave feeling that your time has been wasted. That is not good for you or for the organization.

The positive energy we receive when we help others literally vibrates through our minds and souls, and sends positive energy to those around us. When we are happy, we work harder and are willing to give more. When people see that, they are drawn to us because they want to be around happy people who work hard. People hire and work with people they like. Here is an added bonus: your next client or director may be among those with whom you have worked in this volunteer setting. Because you take this work – for which you have not been paid – so seriously and execute projects with such passion, these "hiring managers" know that you will be untouchable in a professional setting in which you are being compensated.

I volunteer with organizations that I can learn new skills to use later and where I may utilize the skills I currently have. I love politics and am an attorney, so I volunteer with organizations that are politically affiliated and those that serve indigent legal clients. However, as I have become busier with family, work, and other responsibilities, my time for volunteerism has become restricted. Therefore, I donate a bit more to help organizations that I support to recruit volunteers who have more time and provide more resources to do their work. But remember: money cannot compensate you for the missed opportunities to work alongside and network with those who share your zeal for a certain cause.

Save 10%. Save yourself. Save time everyday to rejuvenate your body, settle your mind, and renew your heart and soul. Ten percent of 24 hours is 2.4 hours (or 144 minutes) that may be divided any way you like. Here is how you can get it in:
• Every morning before you get moving, take 30 minutes to quiet your mind and give thanks for another day. Meditate or pray on

empowering messages and motivating sounds. Note things that come to you during this time in your journal.

- Exercise your body everyday at least 45 minutes. A thirty minute walk or jog and 15 minute stretch or strength routine helps relieve the stress of both your mind and body.
- Every evening before you go to bed, reserve 30 minutes to settle your mind, clearing it of the day's events. Reflect on what you learned, not on mistakes made. Be grateful for all the good that came your way – and that you sent to others. Note things that come to you during this time in your journal, meditate or pray over them, and let the day go.
- Take two 5 minute breaks during the day to SOW so you may reap good work: Stretch your arms and legs to limber you up, take three or four deep breaths to Oxygenate your mind, and drink a bottle of Water to hydrate your skin.
- With your remaining 30 minutes (I rounded up from 29 – you are worth that extra minute!), do something you truly enjoy. I enjoy reading, writing, planning outings with my family and friends. Whatever you do during this time, make it something FUN and ENJOYABLE.

Live on 80%. Eighty percent of 24 hours is A LOT of time – 19.2 hours to be exact. Sonja Natasha Brown, creator of Designed for Destiny says that each of us was designed for a certain purpose or destiny. So during the 19.2 hours you have to enjoy, live the best life you can – by design, not by accident.

Life is to be enjoyed, not endured. So how do you do this? As a leader of many, you must start first by leading yourself. First, get enough rest everyday – six to eight hours. Second, spend quality (not quantity) time with your loved ones on a consistent basis – if you do not have a spouse and/or children, or relatives nearby, spend time with your extended family and friends. Third, take affirmative and specific steps toward fulfilling the goals expressed on your vision board. Next, live within your means – make a realistic budget that includes savings goals and stick to it. Also, work hard and be focused when you are at work, but leave work at work. Last, play just as hard as you work. You work to live, not the other way around.

Conclusion

Thank you for going on this journey with me. I hope you found the advice herein useful and that you will find some ways to incorporate some of what I have shared on your journey. I also hope you know others who could benefit from it. If so, please pass it on! Finally, I would love to hear from you! Feel free to reach out to me on my website: **www.LynitaMitchellBlackwell.com**.

ABOUT THE AUTHOR

Lynita Mitchell-Blackwell is a writer, attorney, CPA, facilitator, and speaker who has served in several leadership positions – professional, civic, political and social – and manages her own law firm. Ms. Mitchell-Blackwell also co-founded a non-profit leadership and professional development training organization that she managed for four years and for which she was awarded the 2012 President's Call to Service Award by the Council on Service and Civic Participation.

Ms. Mitchell-Blackwell is a blogger of politics and social issues with the Atlanta Urban League Young Professionals *Politicker*, writer for the AME Church Women's Missionary Society *Workbook*, and was a columnist for *My Magazine for Girls* for three years.

A 2011 *Black Enterprise Magazine* "Next 35" Young & Bold Business Leader and self-proclaimed political junkie, Ms. Mitchell-Blackwell enjoys running, reading, writing, and trying new things. She lives with her family in Atlanta.

www.ingramcontent.com/pod-product-compliance
Lightning Source LLC
Chambersburg PA
CBHW060100050426
42448CB00011B/2548